NOW, ABOUT THAT BUDGET...

NOW, ABOUT THAT BUDGET...

Contemplations, Meditations,
and Affirmations

on

How to, at Least,
Start Thinking About Creating a Budget at Any Age

Sibongile B.N. Lynch

...Lula (Hale) Williams, Ibaye

Copyright © 2024 by Sibongile B. N. Lynch

Published in the United States by
Wynnbrook Press, Clayton County, Georgia
persistence12@gmail.com

First Printing, 2024

The moral rights of the author have been asserted.

All rights reserved. No part of this publication may be reproduced, in whole or in part, in any form (beyond that permitted by Sections 107 and 108 of the U.S. Copyright Law and except by reviewers for the public press), without permission from the publisher.

CONTENTS

PREFACE	1
INTRODUCTION	5
FOUNDATION	8
TRUST	9
GRATITUDE	11
FAITH	13
ACTION	16
STUDY	17
DISCIPLINE/SACRIFICE	19
GIVING	21
CREATIVITY	23
STEADFASTNESS	25
CONFIDENCE	27
AFTERWORD	28
ACKNOWLEDGEMENTS	32
ABOUT THE AUTHOR	33

I wrote this little book, primarily, for women who are either retired or about to retire, and think that it is too late to start saving or creating wealth. However, anyone who find the ideas of budgeting, saving, and investing to be daunting, just know that you are not alone, and you too might benefit from some of the thoughts and notions in these pages. If you are still working or have an income of any kind, it is not too late to build wealth. Now, you may not get rich quick! But you will learn that there is no lack or limitation when you chose to live with a mindset of abundance, and believe that it is available to you. Now, I will not tell you how much of your income you need to save, or throw a bunch of numbers at you, or tell you that you're doomed if you don't see things my way. This is not a book to tell you *how* to budget your money—only you know that. I simply want to give you hope. It is my desire that you will, at least, consider the possibilities with just a simple change in the way you see wealth—and life.

PREFACE

For most, the road to creating wealth for yourself is often an ambitious endeavor. Whether you work at a job or career that you love, and that pays well— or one that doesn't—saving can be a challenge. In our society, some form of income is required to meet your own personal needs and goals. But if you are a parent, you need a second job to meet the needs of your children; one for your fur baby, one to contribute to organizational affiliations, or siblings who are struggling; and at least, one more for miscellaneous needs and wants. This is especially true if you are a woman over 60, in or near retirement, who is either single or widowed. Perhaps you want to retire—log off the proverbial time clock for good—but what feels like a persistent barrage of monetary demands never seem to let up. There's just always something.

It has taken me some time to learn to how to start changing my relationship to money. I no longer see the acquisition of money simply as a means to get material goods or services. Of course, some form of money is necessary in our society to meet some of our basic needs. But having access to the things you want and desire has more to do with the ways in which you perceive and utilize money. And maybe even more importantly how you realize your Self and your place in the world. Developing your consciousness on a level beyond the material, beyond the physical, will help you gain a sense of security that can't be shaken by the latest designer handbag.

I grew up in a working-class neighborhood. My family was not poor, but we were not middle-classed either. Fortunately, I was still in elementary school when Sassoon jeans became all the rage. And anyway, I was what some considered a chubby kid, and back then, designer clothes did not come in all sizes. Additionally, my mother was rather frugal, and for the most part, was a stay-at-home mom with four daughters. My father worked as an officer at a medium security institution in St. Louis, Missouri, and was the sole provider for our family. Eating out was a luxury that only few experienced in our neighborhood. And when we were occasionally treated to a sack of ten cent White Castles, that was a big deal. We had a home, we ate good; and only once I remember our electricity going out.

My dream of traveling the world, I believe, started when I was a kid exploring my neighborhood at during the time when kids could leave the house, and their parents trusted that they would return in one piece. I would ride my bicycle across many city blocks, and be back in time for dinner. As an adult I have traveled to Trinidad, London, and Morocco—places my parents could only imagine. But back then, our idea of a vacation was an occasional road trip to Little Rock or Detroit to see family. Now, I would spend my last dime to take a trip somewhere far away—*just ask my husband.* So, like you, I am still on this journey of learning how to budget and save money; not just to make one or two purchases, but to secure and maintain a reasonable and comfortable lifestyle for the rest of my earthly life.

INTRODUCTION

If you are struggling with the idea of creating and maintaining a budget in order to save money or create wealth, guess what? You are not alone. For starters, night and day, we are bombarded with stuff. From burgers to Bentleys, products, goods and services are mercilessly dangled before us from the moment we wake up in the morning, until we close our eyes to sleep at night. And that's just the stuff we don't need. I love the monologue that comedian George Carlin performs examining our compulsion to acquire things. He says: "…that's the whole meaning of life, isn't it? Trying to find a place for your stuff. That's all your house is… just a place for your stuff… it's a pile of stuff with a cover on it…"

In addition to the stuff we don't need, are the things that are truly necessary, like shelter, nutrition, healthcare and education, stuff we may actually require in this life. And even if we get the job we need to acquire and maintain those things we deem necessary, we have to spend so much of our lives doing that job, that we often neglect our physical, spiritual, and emotional needs in order to have the products, goods, and services that, we believe, will fill the void of giving over so much of our time to keeping up appearances, in the first place. It is the proverbial, and quintessential, hamster wheel.

But before I get too far ahead of myself, let me disclaim: I am not a psychologist, a minister, or financial guru in any shape, form, or fashion. Any suggestions I give regarding saving or investing is simply that, a suggestion; and it should not be construed as professional or legal advice. I was an English major in college. I don't even consider myself to be that good with numbers. But if, like me, you've struggled with creating a budget, or if you have concerns about a dwindling savings, or if you're wondering if you'll be able to take care of yourself as you age, or if you fear you may have to return to the workforce when you're 75—these simple contemplations, meditations, and affirmations may help you think differently about your money. If you begin to think differently about the necessity and usefulness of currency, you may be more open to the possibility of creating a plan for the money and wealth you already have. In fact, I won't even tell you how or when to make a budget; and, I won't ask you about your finances or tell you to stop enjoying your life. It is my desire to help you change your relationship to and understanding of money by focusing on the things that are truly more important.

FOUNDATION

TRUST

"All of my needs are met."

Thanks to Michael Bernard Beckwith, founder of Agape International Spiritual Center in Los Angeles, this affirmation has infiltrated my cells and atoms, and it calms me when my trust occasionally waivers. I say it quietly to myself when I open my eyes every morning. I say it throughout the day. And now, I even greet my husband with, "All of our needs are met." There is no lack or limitation in my life. That's not to say I presently have a lot of stuff, go a lot of places, or do a lot of things. I have a modest home, an unpretentious vehicle. And we mostly cook at home. Both my husband and I are retired, and enjoy reasonably good health for our ages—some might even say, exceptional. We live in a healthy environment with green grass, beautiful trees, and fresh air. I do not take these things for granted, for there are many in the world who dream about such a life. My life is not always exciting. I am at an age now where excitement is not a requirement. But I am happy. Over the years my life has become progressively more secure, both financially and emotionally.

So, just try it. Try to intuit, at all times, that "All of your needs are met." It's not magic. Do you often lament that, "I am broke," "I can't," "I wish I could…" "I'll never have enough money to…"? Stop it! Words and thoughts have energy. Has there ever been a person in your life who you didn't have to question? If they say they are going to do something, you could bet money on it because you know they'll come through. Bet on yourself in that same way. Begin to think, and see the possibilities! Even if you can't *see* them just yet. Work toward your goals, and stop trying to make things happen. They will happen in Divine order and Divine time.

GRATITUDE

(I) Give Thanks.

Have you ever sat or walked quietly, and simply said or thought: Give thanks, I give thanks? I don't mean, "I give thanks" *to* a deity, or a person, or anything your imagination might conjure. But have you ever just taken moments to *be* grateful, to sit in appreciation, not for any-*thing*, but simply for the purpose of putting the energy of gratitude out into the universe. Before we even begin to think about all the things we have or the things we've done, we must give thanks for even the air that we breathe. Isn't it amazing? You don't even have to think about how to breathe; and you don't stop breathing when you go to sleep at night. You just breathe—in, out, inhale, exhale. It's a miracle! The old folks in the Baptist church that I grew up in, when they prayed, they'd say things like: "Lord, thank you for letting me see a day that I've never seen before." As young folks, we somehow thought that was funny, but it was truly profound. Or, they'd say: "Lord, if you never grant me another blessing, I thank you've for all you already done."

Think about your life. What have you overcome? What have you achieved? What have you experienced that did not take you out? *Be* grateful. Consider that you have a home— rented or owned— though it may not be the biggest or newest. You are protected from the elements. However you have managed to acquire or maintain it—it is yours. You have food to eat, and even if it is only beans and rice every day, it sustains you and helps to keep you alive. And you have people who love and care for you, whether biologically related, related by marriage, or the family we choose, you are loved. Particularly in the United States, we have more than most people in the world. To many, we are rich simply because of our location and place of birth. Know that you are so blessed! You are so grateful!

FAITH

God is the source of my supply.

By now, surely you have noticed that many of my ideas and viewpoints geared toward creating a positive and productive attitude about money and budgeting, admittedly, are inspired by my spiritual and religious background. I can't help it. At the risk of coming off too churchy, I confess, I believe in Divine Spirit; the presence that is never in absence—something way bigger than us, but that permeates all of life. I believe in Cosmic Energy and Creative Intelligence—*insert your preferred title here*_____. But even if that Divine Presence, whatever you call it, in which you believe is your Self, hold on to that. For whatever you need, God is the source of your supply. Your job is the conduit of that source, through which you receive the funds to acquire all of those needs. But even if you currently have no job, however you receive the things you need to keep you alive, keep you feed and clothed, those things have been provided—even if it is through a charity of some sort. And each day that you are above ground and animated, you always have the opportunity to make tomorrow a better day. If you are conscious and have a mind, you can tap into Divine Creativity and Divine Intelligence to rise above your circumstances. You can use your mind to imagine not simply a better life, but a comfortable, happy, and secure rest of your life. In *The Living Bible*, in the book of Hebrews, it says that faith is, "…the confident assurance that something we want is going to happen. It is the certainty that what we hope for is waiting for us, even though we cannot see it up ahead." Can you sustain that kind of confidence long enough to put money aside, and fight the temptation to buy that thing you absolutely don't need because you think you deserve to treat yourself? Growing up in church, we heard the twentieth verse of the Book of James recited as, "…faith without works is dead." But the *New Living Translation Bible*, in my opinion, expresses it in such a way as cannot be mistaken: "…Can't you see that faith without good deeds is useless?" If you're waiting for a windfall, spoiler alert: It won't happen. Believing that your finances will improve without taking the steps to make that improvement happen is useless.

ACTION

STUDY

*I will learn the strategies of the Jones'
who save and invest.*

We have all heard the saying, "Keeping up with the Joneses." Well, who are the "Joneses? But more importantly, are you trying to keep up with them by spending money needlessly in order to take on the accoutrements of the wealthy? We all know those people who always seem to have the latest fashion, the newest automobile, the biggest house on the block; and yet, they struggle to pay for the necessities. The phrase, "Keeping up with the Jones'", stems from a 1910 comic strip of the same name by Arthur R. Momand, "depicting the social climbing McGinnis family, who struggle to "keep up" with their neighbors, the Joneses." Are you any less deserving than the Joneses? Of course not. We've also heard the saying, "Not all money is good money," and we have no idea how the Joneses can afford the things they have. Sure, the Joneses may enjoy a great career with an enviable compensation, or just maybe, they have established practices of budgeting, saving, and investing in order to build their wealth. But here's the thing: Despite what you see on your television, you usually can't tell who the truly wealthy people are just by looking at their outward appearance. For example, do you know what designer Warren Buffett usually wears? Neither do I because Mr. Buffett didn't become a billionaire by wearing someone else' name on his shirts. Yet, when it comes to investing, Warren Buffett is considered the GOAT (Greatest Of All Time). Instead of trying to *look* like the Joneses, learn the money management practices of the *real* Joneses who budget, save, and invest. Stop trying to appear wealthy to people who don't matter anyway, and be wealthy.

DISCIPLINE/SACRIFICE

*I resist the temptation to succumb
to compulsive behavior.*

The word discipline, I know, it just sounds like something painful, right? It sounds as though you will be punished for something terrible that you should not have done. As someone who has struggled with weight issues for most of my life, trying to control what I eat often feels like I am denying myself something that is a basic necessity. (Yes, sometimes ice cream is a necessity.) But there are things I need, and there are things I want. It is a mark of maturity to be able to distinguish between the two, and make the sacrifice for our future goals. There will always be a new movie to see, or the latest fashion craze. A new restaurant in town is calling your name; not to mention your friends are insisting that you go out for a night on the town. It's frustrating to deny yourself these small pleasures in life, even when you know you will win in the end. That $50 dollars you save and put in a high yield savings account may only earn you $2.50 this month, but think of all the times you've spent $50 dollars and what that could've been in a year. Not to mention the compounding interest—"*forget about it.*"

British author, James Allen, wrote: "He who would accomplish little must sacrifice little; he who would achieve much must sacrifice much; he who would attain highly must sacrifice greatly." Start slowly, and create routines, such as, jotting down on a notepad all the things you purchase in a day. Form a habit of adding those things up at the end of the day to see just where your money is going. Just as the coronavirus began to spread, (and I was fortunate enough to work from home), I used an online banking tool to calculate how much I was spending every morning for that grande latte with an extra shot of espresso. It showed that I'd spent over $1,000 for the previous year! The pandemic was a good time to start making my coffee at home, and now, I rarely buy coffee out. Small sacrafices add up, and you must trust that it won't be that way forever.

GIVING

I am blessed to be a blessing.

There is a universal law called the *law of reciprocity*. You participate in this law when you practice random acts of kindness. When your grass needs attention, and you look out your window to see your neighbor mowing your lawn, even though you didn't ask him to; and then, you make him a pan of your tasty lasagne that you know he enjoys so much. That is reciprocity. Many of us learned about tithing and offering in church. So, we already know that being a blessing to someone will yield us a blessing in return somewhere down the line. When you give you express to the universe that you have it to give, and that you are willing to share what you have. The universe, in turn, continues to pour into you, so that you may continue to bless others. Some may also consider this the *law of circulation*. The return blessing may not always be what you expect, or when you expect it, but it will come back.

If your hands are always closed into a fist because you are holding on so tight to what little you have, they'll never be open to receive. Generousity goes a long way. And giving doesn't always mean ten percent. Give what you can, when you can, as often as you can. "Give and it shall be given unto you."

CREATIVITY

I create my own beautiful world!

Sometimes as adults we forget how much fun it was to do the simple things we did as children. Whether playing in the grass amongst the butterflies in the summer, or making snow angels in the winter, these kinds of activities allowed us to explore our imaginations. But then we grow up, get a job, and by the time we get home from work, the only thing we can imagine is the inside of our eyelids. But, if *necessity is the mother of invention*, what might creativity be the mother of?

The next time you find yourself frustrated because you've been disciplining yourself, sacraficing, saving, and giving, think outside the box. When was the last time you put together a puzzle with the family? Sure, you could turn on the television and watch a movie, but try a new recipe, and you might discover that you have a talent for baking cakes —which you turn into a business. Or, perhaps, you write beautiful poetry for which someone will pay you for to give to a loved one. Maybe coloring in a coloring book will help you focus your mind, which allows you to find the answers to the problems you once thought mounumental.

A relative in Trinidad asked me to bring a grounding mat the last time I traveled there. A grounding mat is a conductive device that mimics the effects of walking barefoot on the earth by creating an electrical connection between your body and the ground. But I thought, why not just go outside and walk in the grass barefoot? So since I retired from my job where I sat in flourescent lit offices for twenty years, I've been going outside in my backyard barefoot, breathing fresh air, taking in the warm summer sun, and communing with nature. It is a beautiful and relaxing way to center yourself in the universe, and open up that childhood imagination you once enjoyed.

STEADFASTNESS

I won't falter, even when others can't understand my path.

So here you are, sacraficing, saving, and walking barefoot in your yard talking to the trees. Your good friend wants you to take an impromptu trip to Jamaica. It's her birthday, and it just would't be the same without you. But your emergency fund has been earning interest, and is finally enough for you to live on should you find yourself without a job for three months—*and* it's for emergencies. Is Jamaica an emergency? These temptations will happen. Friends will be disappointed because instead of spending recklessly for an unplanned vacation, you've chosen to invest in yourself and your future. But it's important that you stay focused. Real friends will understand.

Besides, in your studying and research, you've discovered new associations who share the same goals and path as you. This has allowed you to learn even more about budgeting, saving, and investing. And with your new friends, you'll share new and creative ideas for inexpensive, or even free, entertainment. So, do not be deterred by those who can't understand or encourage your path, or your growth.

CONFIDENCE

*I can do all things through Divine Spirit
that strengthens me.*

By now, I hope that you are considering some of the things discussed in this little book. I hope that you are, at least, starting to think about the possibility of securing a better future for yourself by making small changes. I know, it is often a challenge when you are trying to make adjustments to the way you've been used to doing things. But if you just take that first step, you will at least learn something new.

Just know that you are a whole and complete person without the material baubles that society and advertising try to convince you to consume. Strengthen your resolve through prayer and meditation. And using your creativity, envision your life the way you desire it to be, and work towards the things that are truly important: love, joy, peacefulness, family, strong relationships, and the knowledge that you can do all things through Divine Spirit.

AFTERWORD

I told you that I wouldn't ask you about your finances or ask you to write anything down. But here are some helpful hints and ideas to help you get started while you are *just thinking* about creating a budget that will work for you.

1) First, close your eyes, and just envision the kind of life you truly want to live. What does it look like? How does it feel?

2) Get a pad of paper and causually jot down what you spend each day. Add it all up, and compare at the end of the week, the month, and see where you might possibly make some changes. (Like the daily stop at the coffee shop which will remain nameless.)

3) I learned that there are great communities of women online who are saving, budgeting, and learning to invest and trade. Check out YouTube *University* and type in simple search terms like "women investing," "women saving money," "bud-

geting", etc.

4) Make walking in the park, or walking barefoot in your backyard a new routine. Get in the garden and do some weeding. Greet the birds each morning, and thank the trees for their oxygen.

5) Research online to find banks who offer high yield savings accounts to see which one has the best deal. Chances are you'll find one that pays a lot more than your current banking institution.

6) Anything you can get in a resturant, you can make at home with a simple recipe. There are tons of them online!

7) If you're looking for an easy to use tool to organize your budgeting, I use Google Sheets. I learned to use it watching a YouTube video called: *The Ultimate Google Sheets Budget Template Tutorial for Beginners!*

6) For all things be grateful, and give with a heart as light as a feather.

NOTES

NOTES

ACKNOWLEDGEMENTS

Always, first and foremost, I acknowledge and give thanks to Divine cosmic energy and creative intelligence, present everywhere at all times. And to my muse, for your patience and willingness to be there when I call.

To my husband, for daring to marry an aspiring writer some 24 years ago.

And to poet, Mary Meriam, for your experience and guidance. Thank you for giving me this gift.

ABOUT THE AUTHOR

Sibongile Binta Nonkululeko-Lynch has written for *Black Magnolias*, *The Cygnet,* and *Aunt Chloe* Literary Journals; *Creative Loafing*, and *Georgia* (GEMC) Magazines.

www.sibongilelynch.com

Wynnbrook Press, 2024

Made in the USA
Columbia, SC
13 December 2024